RAILS ACROSS EUROPE

NORTHERN AND WESTERN EUROPE

RAILS ACROSS EUROPE

NORTHERN AND WESTERN EUROPE

DAVID CABLE

Pen & Sword
TRANSPORT

First published in Great Britain in 2016 by
Pen & Sword Transport
An imprint of Pen & Sword Books Ltd
47 Church Street
Barnsley
South Yorkshire
S70 2AS

ISBN 978 1 47384 428 5

Printed and bound in India by Replika Press Pvt. Ltd.

Pen & Sword Books Ltd incorporates the imprints of Pen & Sword Archaeology, Atlas, Aviation, Battleground, Discovery, Family History, History, Maritime, Military, Naval, Politics, Railways, Select, Social History, Transport, True Crime, and Claymore Press, Frontline Books, Leo Cooper, Praetorian Press, Remember When, Seaforth Publishing and Wharncliffe.

For a complete list of Pen & Sword titles please contact
Pen & Sword Books Limited
47 Church Street, Barnsley, South Yorkshire, S70 2AS, England
E-mail: enquiries@pen-and-sword.co.uk
Website: www.pen-and-sword.co.uk

DAVID CABLE – OTHER PUBLICATIONS

Railfreight in Colour (for the modeller and historian)
BR Passenger Sectors in Colour (for the modeller and historian)
Lost Liveries of Privatisation in Colour (for the modeller and historian)
Hydraulics in the West
The Blue Diesel Era
Rails Across North America – A Pictorial Journey Across the USA
Rails Across Canada – A Pictorial Journey Across Canada
Rails Across Europe – Eastern and Southern

Introduction

From the early days of proper railways being developed in England, Railway Mania spread a spider's web of lines throughout Europe, partly financed by speculative business entrepreneurs and partly by communities and states. In many cases, lines were built to keep other companies lines out of an area, the result of which being that many were unremunerative and have subsequently been closed. By the end of the nineteenth century, the network of railways was virtually complete, and it was not until the 1970s that any major new construction took place with the development of High Speed lines in France and Germany, followed by the Channel Tunnel in the 1990s, the connection between the Channel Tunnel and London being opened in the 21st century, and now developments in Poland, Belgium and the Netherlands.

Except for Norway and parts of Scotland and Wales, North and West Europe is generally fairly flat, so that locomotives of moderate power were manufactured of a size able to cope with ever increasing loads, relying on banking engines where sharp gradients necessitated. Apart from the Romanov Empire and Ireland, the standard gauge used in Great Britain, 4' 8½" (1435mm), was adopted, albeit with a larger loading gauge than in the British Isles, which has restricted the use of wagons of the Continental mainlands being able to work on British tracks. Rolling stock moving to and from Russia, the Baltic states and Finland, where the track gauge is 5' 0" (1520mm), have to change bogies, now a fairly quick procedure, whilst the railways in Ireland, which use a 5' 3" (1600mm) gauge, are quite divorced from the rest of Europe. There are, in addition, a number of lines of narrower gauges which serve specific areas, and had the advantage of being cheaper to build. These are seen more in the east than the west of this area of Europe.

Around the end of the nineteenth century, progress was being made in electrifying railways, and this has become widespread on main lines throughout this part of Europe. In the main, overhead wiring systems are used, the exceptions being in the south of England, and most city Metro lines, where 3rd rail pick up is used. OHE voltages vary from 1.5/3 kV DC in Belgium, Netherlands and parts of France, 15kV AC in Germany, Austria and Switzerland), and 25kV elsewhere. With more international through working of trains, locomotives are being increasingly fitted for multi-voltage electrics. Unfortunately, different safety systems in many countries still restrict total flexibility, but EU diktats are starting to resolve this problem.

Passenger services comprise High Speed trains formed of Electric Multiple Unit sets, main line expresses mainly hauled by locomotives, local services also using EMUs, and city Metro services. Main line services still provide food of some sort, but sleeping cars have largely disappeared since the speeds of trains now largely complete journeys in daylight hours. Freight services are all loco hauled, and these have developed widely into Trans European workings carrying bulk loads and containers, rather than individual wagon type services. As a result, most small local freight yards have been abandoned. Whereas in former times the railways in each country were either state controlled or were self-contained corporations, the last thirty years have seen a marked increase in companies using Open Access opportunities to gain business from the larger units, often taking some of the more profitable work.

Northern European electric locomotives are now predominantly built by five manufacturers, Alstom, Bombardier, PESA, Siemens and Vossloh with General Motors/EMD having major penetration with diesel locomotives and power units. Locos have increased in power over the years, and have become increasingly sophisticated with multi-voltage and safety equipment adding to costs, such that several rail companies, particularly the Open Access groups, prefer to lease locos rather than purchase them outright. The leasing companies have included Dispolok, MRCE, Railpool and ELL, whilst in Great Britain, all rolling stock is leased from the ROSCO rolling stock finance houses. Other rolling stock has tended to increase in size, particularly freight wagons, which are now almost all carried on bogies. Coaching stock is somewhat longer, with more facilities for disabled persons, but less room for passengers' luggage, and often seats which do not line up with windows. Trains for local workings and suburban areas almost all now are fitted with sliding doors.

So in the twenty-first century, the situation in North and West Europe is that several countries still have state subsidised and controlled railways, whereas others have split their operations into business sectors under an overall umbrella, and some have privatised their systems into various profit making franchises.

The purpose of this book is to show a selection of classes, locations and colour schemes in the different countries that have been seen over the last thirty years. The pictures in this book are almost all of my own, taken during holidays and business trips over the last thirty years, supported by some photos taken by my friend, Murray Lewis, who has visited places to which I have not been, and for which I thank him. A few photos in my collection were taken by Steve Sachse (now deceased), who left no details of the subjects. Detective work by Brian Garvin and Keith Fender has filled in most gaps, for which I thank them as well. Some of my pictures from the 1970s were taken on film of dubious manufacture and quality. I apologise for these, but since they are of sufficient historic interest, I have done my best with Photoshop to make them worthy of inclusion.

Whereas in Britain, there is a publication showing rostered freight working details at various points in the country, enabling identification of particular trains, as well as normal passenger timetables, no such information has been available for me to use for freight trains in mainland Europe, so details on these are less than sparse, which I regret.

This volume should be read in conjunction its sister volume, *Rails Across Europe – Eastern and Southern*. The section on Great Britain is minimal, since a future volume on that country is in the course of preparation.

David Cable
Hartley Wintney, Hants, UK
April 2015

Notes on railways of each country

Belgium

The railways in Belgium are state owned, SNCB being the operator. International services from Paris work through Belgium to Amsterdam and Koln, and Eurostar services from London terminate in Brussels. All main lines are electrified. Freight services from the port of Antwerp are worked into Germany and France.

Denmark

Although the main system DSB is state owned, there are many privately operated short lines throughout this country. Regular services work through to Malmo in Sweden, and freight services operate into Germany. Although there is some electrification, diesel operated trains form many services.

Estonia

Railways are of the Russian broad gauge, with a limited number of passenger services operated by multiple units, plus overnight services to and from Russia. Heavy freight trains, especially oil for export, work through from Russia to the docks at Tallinn. Ed Burkhardt, formerly of Wisconsin Central, established freight operations using ex-USA diesel locomotives, which have now been absorbed into the state system.

Finland

The Finnish railways are state owned and also use the Russian gauge. Services are almost all electrically operated, with a mixture of locomotive hauled and multiple unit stock, all of fairly modern designs.

France (North)

This book covers the part of France north of a line from Strasbourg to Nantes. The old individual railways were nationalised by the state forming SNCF, which dominates operations, and militant Trade Unionism causes frequent interruptions to day-to-day activities, also making open access introduction particularly difficult in this country. France pioneered the use of High Speed lines in Europe with the well-known TGV trains. Photos of trains in the south of France are shown in the companion volume, *Rails Across Europe – Eastern and Southern*.

Germany

The former individual state railways were amalgamated before the Second World War into a national system, but following this conflict, railways in the West (DB) and East (DR) of the country operated independently until the country was re-united. Trains were developed independently, and it was significant that two highly regarded classes of East German design, the classes 143 and 155, were transferred into DB areas very quickly after unification. Trains run between Germany and several other

European countries, with many of their locomotive designs being used. The DB Schenker sector has taken over operations in a number of countries, including Great Britain, Poland, Romania and Bulgaria. German railways have some of the most intensive services in Northern Europe, but in recent times, their enviable reputation for punctuality has developed cracks. Germany is now host to many regional and private train companies operating both passenger and freight services.

Great Britain

From the myriad of companies existing up to the First World War, four major companies were formed, which in 1948 were nationalised into British Rail. In the 1990s, the UK government decided to privatise the railways, franchising different lines and areas to a range of train operators, particularly bus companies, whilst having a separate organisation to maintain the tracks. Many franchises have been sold on, and there has been a major increase in passenger usage, but very little increase in freight train activity. More details will be given in the forthcoming book on the railways of Great Britain.

Ireland

The railways in the Irish Republic and Northern Ireland work in close harmony, with international services between Dublin and Belfast. With the exception of commuter services around the two capital cities, passenger services are somewhat widespread, serving the major towns and cities fairly infrequently, and freight trains are scarce. Multiple units are starting to dominate passenger services.

Latvia and Lithuania

Like Estonia, these two countries use the Russian broad gauge. Rolling stock is predominantly of Russian design, and train services reflect both internal and through services to and from Russia, particularly via Lithuania to the Russian enclave on the Baltic Sea at Kaliningrad.

Luxemburg

Largely self-contained, the railway is mainly electrified, but with some passenger services working to Belgium, France and Germany. Freight services are of an international nature. Rolling stock has been recently modernised, and the system works effectively. CFL now also operates freight services in Scandinavia.

Netherlands

With frequent electric passenger services throughout the country, and with regular workings into both Belgium and Germany, the state owned Dutch railways also provide an intensive freight service to and from the major dock facilities in the Rotterdam area, particularly with import/export activities from across mainland Europe. However, international services from Amsterdam and Hoek van Holland as far afield as Moscow and Innsbruck have largely been curtailed.

Norway

The terrain of Norway has meant that railways in this country have had to take sometimes difficult routes between centres of populations, and the need for tracks often to be single with passing loops, restricts the frequency of services.

Passenger trains are formed of both loco hauled and multiple unit train sets operated by the state owned system. Freight operations are handled by two freight operating companies.

Poland

The railways of Poland host trains operated by a large number of private operators in addition to the national company sectors. A wide range of old and new rolling stock can be seen, several types having been obtained from other countries, particularly the Czech Republic, with many locos of Russian manufacture still present. Polish trains can now be seen as far afield as the Netherlands and Austria on freight services, whilst regular passenger services operate into Germany, Czech Republic and

Slovakia, whilst freight trains are worked into Belarus and Ukraine with bogie changing at the borders. High Speed trains now use special tracks between Warszawa and Krakow/Katowice.

Russia
The few photos taken in Russia in this volume only give a brief insight into this country's trains, but the sheer size of the Russian loading gauge, and the imposing double locomotives in their wide range of colour schemes are noteworthy.

Sweden
In addition to the state owned railways, there are a substantial number of private operating companies working both passenger and freight services. The Swedish railways use indigenous designs of locomotives in the main, although some leased engines from German companies are starting to intrude. The X2000 EMUs still provide an efficient fast InterCity service supplemented by loco hauled main line and EMU operated suburban service. Internal freight services are worked by the Green Cargo sector, whilst Hector Rail in particular has developed international freight services into Germany with some success.

N.B. No photographs of trains in Belarus have been available for this volume, but they are, of course, very similar to those of Russia.

Belgium
The SNCB class 18 was identical to the 4-voltage SNCF class 40100. Belgian 1802 is ready to leave Paris Nord in April 1988 with an express to Koln.

Brightening up Ostend station in May 1991, three clean locos are stabled ready for their next duties. They are 1601, 1501 and 1603, all of multi-voltage classes. Both classes were built by BN.

Based on the AFB design with GM engines, a pair of fifty-three class locos, 5316 and 5306 head north through Namur station with a mixed freight train.

Dual voltage Class 25 2557 speeds through Schaarbeek in the Brussels outskirts, with a Paris Nord to Amsterdam express, taking advantage of the super-elevated curve.

One of the class 11s, which worked the jointly operated trains between Brussels and Amsterdam, passes Mechelen Nekkerspoel on its way from Amsterdam to Brussels Midi. The whole train is in the special colours designated for these services. This class was developed from the class 21, with dual voltage provided.

Antwerp Centraal station as it used to be in May 1991, with AM86 EMU 914 awaiting departure and class 62 6295 passing the time. Due to their design, the units were nicknamed Snorkels.

Antwerp Dam diesel shed on a Sunday afternoon, hosting a variety of locomotives including 5175, 5158, 8417 and 8516.

The magnificent battlements at Ghent station rather overwhelm class 62 6304 ready to leave for Eeklo in May 1991. These locos were also built by BN using GM diesel engines.

Class 20 2002 exits the tunnels under the city and approaches Brussels Nord with an express from Brussels Midi to Basel in September 1994. This class of twenty-five locomotives was the only electric Co-Co type on SNCB.

Preserved AFB class 54 5404 makes a nice surprise at Namur one late afternoon in September 1994, where it is seen working a Namur to Dinant service, with steam heating working well.

One of the older electric classes (built 1953-54) is represented by class 22 2229, which is bringing an empty stock train into Brussels Midi station in April 2004.

Through working by locomotives into other countries becomes more common, and is illustrated by SNCB class 13 1332 passing through Thionville station in France in May 2004 with a southbound intermodal service.

A line of withdrawn locos, headed by 2624, enjoys the sunshine at Arlon. The class 26 featured monomotor bogies.

SNCB class 13 1317 and CFL class 3000 3018 join forces and pass Noertzange in Luxemburg with an eastbound train of coal hoppers.

Class 21 2159 propels its train out of Berchem with an Antwerp Centraal to Ostend train in May 2004. The class 21 was a lower powered version of the similar looking class 27, which were introduced in the 1980s.

The newer classes of locos have now taken over the Brussels to Amsterdam services, as shown by class 28 2803 (TRAXX class 186) bringing the empty stock into Brussels Midi in August 2012. Note the decorative colour scheme on the coaching stock.

The latest class of loco on the Belgian system is the class 1900, 1907 of which is at Brussels Midi with an Ostend to Eupen service in August 2012.

Denmark

Nohab class MY 1126 works a freight train at Holstebro on an unknown date. The livery is very much non-standard.
(DC Collection)

Class MZ 1431 stands at Rodby Faerge connecting with a ferry. This is a train destined for Kobenhavn in August 1979. (DC Collection)

MA class DMUs, based on the German TEE sets, were used on Lyntog (Lightning) Inter City services between Kobenhavn and Jutland. The set is at either Korser or Nyborg in July 1988. (DC Collection)

DSB MX class 1021 carries a very colourful paint job as it sits in the sun at Kobenhavn in July 1989. (DC Collection)

An ET class EMU 4303 stands at Malmo, Sweden, with a service to Helsingor, Denmark, in September 2003.

In the latest livery, GM diesel powered ME class 1532 leaves the main station in Kobenhavn with an evening commuter service in September 2003.

ME 1518 propels its train away from Hoje Taastrup as it makes its way to Kobenhavn.

The striking station at Hoje Taastrup hosts ME class 1504, which is working a westbound passenger service. The loco carries the older colour scheme.

With an S-bahn EMU waiting to return to the capital city area, ME class 1501 stops at Hoje Taastrup.

In Gods colours, EG class 3107 speeds through Hoje Taastrup with an eastbound mixed freight train glinting in the setting sun.

Electric loco class EA 3006 starts away from Hoje Taastrup with an afternoon passenger train heading west.

An empty class MFA DMU 5078 passes Vesterport in the Kobenhavn suburbs in September 2003.

EG class 3101 arrives at Padborg in July 2005 with a mixed freight train, from which it will uncouple, making way for a German loco to take the train on south. The freight Gods livery is clearly shown in this shot.

Estonia
ED Russian built TEP70 0304 arrives at Tallinn with an overnight sleeper service from Moscow in June 2004. The small piece of roofing is the only cover against the weather at this capital city's terminus.

A close up shot of the TEP70 shows the very neat design of this class of diesel locomotive.

The stock of the Moscow to Tallinn sleeper has been pulled clear of the platforms by ED Czech built CHME3 3141, a design built in thousands, and seen extensively across Eastern Europe in Soviet days.

ED DR18 class DMU 3714 stands at Tallinn in June 2004 with a train for Rapla.

ER ex-Conrail C30-7A 1576 and 1560 pass through Raasiku station with an eastbound freight train in June 2004.

ER Russian built 2TE116 696 passes Raasiku with a westbound train of oil tanks.

ER ex-Union Pacific C36-7 1545 heads a lengthy westbound oil train past Raasiku.

ER 2TE 116 1677 returns to Russia to fill its train with more oil for export through Estonia. It is seen at Raasiku in June 2004, passing a superb old water tower.

Finland

Diesel shunter 1987 pulls a rake of empty coaching stock out of Helsinki station in July 1986. (DC Collection)

Russian built class Sr1 3102 is ready to depart from Helsinki station with the overnight service to Moscow in June 2005.

Sr2 3245 brings a rake of mixed single and double deck empty stock into Helsinki. This class of locomotive is similar to the SBB class 460, and besides Switzerland, this design can also be seen in Norway and Malaysia. The double deck coaches have an interesting fitment – a dumb waiter, which can move a food buffet trolley between the upper and lower decks.

A pair of Sm2 EMUs wait at Helsinki for their departure authorisation, unit 6093 on the right being in the now superseded colour scheme.

Sr2 3203 stops at Tampere with a Turku to Tampere service in June 2005.

Sm3 EMU 7609 arrives at Tampere with a service from Helsinki to Oulu. This class is a Pendolino tilting train unit developed from the Italian ETR460.

Alstom built Sm4 class EMU 6312 sits in the middle of Riihimaki station, with nothing particular to do in June 2005.

Sr1 3084 is in charge of a short northbound container train at Riihimaki.

Sr1 3097 enters Riihimaki with a double deck train from Helsinki to Joensuu.

Very clean diesel shunter 2567 runs light past Riihimaki in June 2005. This loco is of class DV12.

France (North)

One of the electric locos introduced by the PLM post Second World War, using Buchli drive, 2-Do-2 9005 stands by the turntable at Paris Charolais roundhouse in June 1984.

Of a class introduced in 1971 for fast express services, BB15063 *Verdun* departs from Paris Est with an express for Strasbourg in October 1987.

One of the Turbo units T2048 catches the sun after arrival from Caen in October 1987. The train is seen at Paris St Lazare.

In the 1980s, older classes were still in action on minor duties in various locations. At Paris Austerlitz, BB305 removes the empty stock of an express from Bordeaux, which had been brought in behind CC6524 *Toulouse*.

A TGV in the original orange colours stands in Paris Gare de Lyon after arrival from Lyon in October 1987. Note that the corporate initials are carried on the power car. Personally, I much preferred this design of power car with the 'hump' not blended into the cab roof – it gives a better impression of speed.

Centre cab electric BB12015 passes through Aulnay sous Bois with a northbound freight train in April 1988.

One of the four voltage electric locos CC40103 *Brioude* is ready to depart from Paris Nord to Koln.

The Montparnasse Tower dominates the station, where BB8590 is leaving with a train of double deck coaching stock.

A Paris metro train is seen somewhere in the city in April 1988. The rubber tyred and guiding wheels are clearly shown. The centre coach of the five car set is that for first-class passengers.

One of the superb class 15000 locos, BB15051 *Aulnoye-Aymeries,* awaits the departure signal at Strasbourg to start its train to Paris Est in May 1996.

In the special livery for suburban services from Paris Nord, BB 16113 is about to leave the terminus with a train to Amiens in May 1996.

St Malo station in September 1997 displays BB 67304 which will be working through with a stopping service to Rennes.

TGV-A 356 enters the station at St Brieuc with an express from Brest to Paris Montparnasse in September 1997.

BB22392 *Charles Tellier* moves empty stock out of the station at Rennes, ignored by all the young ladies!

In the recently introduced Fret livery, BB425182 trundles through Thionville with a southbound mixed freight train in May 2004. The prefix 4 represents a sector number for the duties to which the locomotive has been allocated.

At the time, a new class of freight locos had been introduced, illustrated by BB427116 at Thionville working a southbound freight train.

On a gloomy morning in Luxemburg, BB115055 waits to leave for Paris Est. The locomotive carries En Voyage colours in May 2004.

In Multiservices livery, BB116021 heads a train to St Quentin, and is seen at Paris Nord in May 2005.

Germany

On an unknown date, DR 118 377-1 brings a train round the curve from the Arnstadt direction and will shortly enter Saalfeld station.

A pair of class 118s stand at the turntable at Wurzburg shed in September 1983. On the left in the original blue colour is 118 050-4. Alongside in the new corporate DB livery is 118 013-2.

During the 1980s, DB introduced services to Frankfurt Airport from two cities, namely Dusseldorf and Stuttgart. The Stuttgart service was operated by a class 111 and, as seen here at Stuttgart Hbf, a class 103 – 103 101-2. The trains carried special white and yellow colours. The Dusseldorf service is depicted further on.

The class 103 was the flagship of DB for many years, and is shown in its original colours at Mainz in January 1988. A northbound express starts off behind 103 107-9, with a matching set of first-class coaches in tow.

The Dusseldorf to Frankfurt Airport service was operated by class 403 EMUs, nicknamed 'Donald Ducks' due to their design and colours. Having caught me unawares, one of these units passes through Mainz Hbf in January 1988.

In May 1994, a Dresden to Zwickau service approaches Chemnitz Hbf behind 156 004-4, still carrying DR identification. This is one of a class of only four locomotives, which were almost exact replicas externally of the DB class 120s, apart from having six wheel bogies. Note the old semaphore signals still at work.

The class 201 to 204 locos were seen extensively on both main and branch lines in the East and later Western Germany. A two coach train is stabled at Juterbog behind 202 549-2 in May 1994.

Seen from the top of the Berlin TV tower, an express train headed by a class 229 'U-Boat' passes a class 475 S-Bahn train near Friedrichstrasse station. Taken in May 1994.

During the 1990s, a number of S-Bahn trains were painted in this colour scheme, including loco classes 111, 141, 143 and the rarer 218. At Nurnberg Hbf, 143 659-1 bathes in the sunshine, ready to leave with an S1 service to Lauf in May 1996.

Trying to get a photo combining rail and river transport together in the Rhine valley is not as easy as one imagines. This effort was taken from the shore at Oberwesel in May 1996, and shows Swiss barge *Alchemist Rom* just within the picture heading upstream, whilst heading north, a pair of class 155s have a mixed freight train in tow.

No need for an excuse to show another picture of a class 103, in this case 103 146-7 approaching Heidelberg with a Stuttgart to Dortmund express, fortunately finding a gap in the overhead wiring on May 1996.

The Siemens built 'Taurus' design for Austria was expanded into a locomotive fleet for leasing under the title Dispolok. At Matrei in Austria on the climb up to the Brenner Pass, ES64 U2 013 and 001 head north with a RoLa train of road vehicles. The locos carry the names of the lessors, but these are unidentified. Taken in June 2002.

The German railways have adopted varieties of special liveries, following the lead of Switzerland, and subsequently Austria and Slovakia. This example shows 101 109-7 advertising Die Marche Italia, a holiday region in Italy. The sun illuminates the Hamburg to Basel express, which stands in Koln Hbf in July 2002.

Private operators have become more widespread on the German network in the twenty-first century. At Rotenburg (Wumme) on a cloudy day in July 2002, a class 232 owned by EVB of Bremervorde, numbered 622.01, comes to a halt at a signal, whilst working west with an intermodal service.

The advertising liveries were very much used on the passenger classes, but 152 084-0 advertised its manufacturer, Siemens, as seen here as it passes through Bremen Hbf with a mixed freight train in July 2002.

In the first part of the twenty-first century, DB introduced a premium business service, which operated between Hamburg and Koln. Two sets of the train were provided, which undertook round trips between these cities, and carried a unique colour scheme. The trains were named Metropolitan. In this photo, one of the two designated locos for these trains, 101 131-1, passes through Munster on its way to Koln, in the evening of a July day in 2002.

Another of the advertising class 101s is seen at Erfurt in June 2003, before the station was rebuilt. 101 078-4 Idee + Spiel heads east with an express from Dusseldorf to Berlin, next stop Weimar. The signal box looks as if it might be somewhat unsteady in a high wind!

One of the unsuccessful ventures into Europe has been the products of General Electric of the USA. The first ten 'Blue Tiger' diesel locos were used by a number of private operators, but no further orders eventuated. The pioneer loco of the class, 250 001-5, passes through Bremen Hbf with a westbound train of coal hoppers in June 2003.

Still in the original freight green colours, 151 003-1 passes Koln Sud with a southbound train of tank wagons in June 2003.

The Rheinbraun system operates trains to feed power stations west of Koln, with indigenous brown coal. It is a totally enclosed system, with a very large loading gauge and special designs of rolling stock, although standard track gauge is used. Showing the full width of one of these trains, loco 502 heads a train of empty coal hoppers returning to the mines, and is seen near Niederaussem in April 2004.

The ICE trains are widespread on main lines throughout Germany, varying in age, design and composition. This class 415/411 train pairing, with 415 505-7 at the rear of a service from Dresden to Frankfurt, is leaving Eisenach in April 2004.

The ThyssenKrupp steelworks at Duisburg dominate the background, whilst in the foreground EuH 522 moves a rake of enclosed coil carriers past a trainload of steel coils in April 2004.

It's all action at Memmingen in July 2004, where 218 240-0 has stopped with a train from Ulm to Oberstdorf, whilst two more class 218s and a pair of class 642 DMUs also hold court in the station.

The MaK DE 2700 class of diesel locos were built for the Norwegian railways as class Di 6, but rejected as unsatisfactory. Having served with Dispolok and being leased to, amongst others, Luxemburg railways, they were tried out by Connex. DE 2700 08 is seen on trials with a Flex Express to Hamburg at Padborg (Denmark), piloting Connex electric loco 185 515 in July 2005.

To my eyes, an extremely pleasant design of engine is the Russian built class 232 series, of which 234 242-6 (a variant with electric train heating) has arrived at Friedrikshafen in May 2006, with a very late running train from Dortmund to Innsbruck.

Grosskorbetha sees a large amount of freight traffic, both using the freight yards or passing through, with both DB and private motive power. Class 228 number 204 owned by Infraleuna arrives with a train of tank wagons in May 2006.

With three Czech coaches forming a Praha to Munchen service and an Arriva Hercules diesel on each end, 223 071-2 is ready to leave Schwandorf where the train reverses, on a beautiful sunny day in April 2008.

A City Night Line train to Amsterdam stops at Koblenz, hauled by ES64 F4 092 leased from MRCE one morning in June 2008.

The Rhine Valley carries many freight trains along the east bank. At Kaub, NF Cargo liveried ES64 F4 093 heads north with an intermodal service.

A direct service that has now been abandoned is seen at Cochem in the Mosel Valley. 181 222-1 has stopped with a Luxemburg to Norddeich Mole express, which will change engines at Koblenz. At 09.58am the train is exactly on time. The date is June 2008.

A Vossloh G2000 class passes Hunfeld with a northbound freight train in July 2008. WLE 21 is privately owned, and is one of this class with a full width cab, whereas the first locos were built with the left-hand end cut back.

A very lucky break came in June 2011 at Rohrbach, where one of the original Vectrons was on its first trial run between Nurnburg and Munchen. 193 902 heads the southbound test train with 101 006-5 bringing up the rear, in case of a problem.

A classic scene at a classic location, Gemunden, where 151 018-9 in DB Railion red speeds south with a well-loaded intermodal train in August 2011.

It is always nice to see an old locomotive brought back into service, as in this example taken at Hilden in August 2013. Operated by BET, 220 053-3 heads a train of aluminium slabs from Spellen to Koblenz.

In August 2013, track work on the normal route to the Netherlands from the Ruhr area meant that many trains were diverted via Venlo. Whilst an ICE from Amsterdam approaches, 120 502 propels a test train towards the Dutch border.

Great Britain

The decision was made in Scotland in the mid-1980s to mark the fleet of main line locomotives used on the predominant Scottish services with the word Scotrail and blue band in place of the standard InterCity scheme. However, the fleet was not always used as intended, as in this example where 47705 *Lothian* is heading a train of empty cement tanks from Uddingston to the Blue Circle works at Oxwellmains, near Dunbar. It is seen here in the outskirts of Dunbar in May 1986.

In South Devon, the railway follows the coast for several miles, providing some very scenic views. A train of empty coaching stock emerges from a tunnel at Horse Cove behind 50015 *Valiant*, still in BR large logo blue in May 1990, with the town of Dawlish in the background.

A train, or iron ore empties, from Llanwern to Port Talbot in South Wales passes Margam behind 37710 and 37884. The locos are in Railfreight grey livery, adorned with metals sector blue and yellow decals. Taken in July 1990.

Class 158 diesel multiple unit 158 713 starts away from its stop at Gleneagles in May 1991. The train is working from Aberdeen to Glasgow Queen Street. The colour scheme is that adopted by the Regional Rails sector for this class.

In full InterCity livery, 91030 *Palace of Holyroodhouse* accelerates south from York on an evening in July 1991, working an Edinburgh to London King's Cross express. The profile of the train allows for tilting, which was never used in practice.

In the 1990s, freight operations were split into three regional operating groups, one of which, Loadhaul, covered the North Eastern part of England. In the striking black and orange with mandatory yellow front end for safety purposes, 56083 passes Monk Fryston with a Merry Go Round coal train from the mine at Gascoigne Wood, to the power station at either Eggborough or Drax. Seen in August 1995.

National Power decided to invest in its own rolling stock to feed its power stations. In this July 1996 view at Whitley Bridge, with Eggborough power station in the background, 59203 *Vale of Evesham* is leaving the power station loop with a trainload of empty wagons, the whole train carrying the NP colour scheme. The company subsequently sold all its rolling stock to EWS.

Conwy Castle was built during the reign of King Edward I during the thirteenth century. Having incredible foresight, the builders left enough space for the two track main line along the North Wales coast to be constructed 600 years later! Seen below the ramparts, a Virgin InterCity 125 High Speed Train (HST) passes on its way from Holyhead to London Euston, with power car 43090 tailing the train. Note that the railway builders constructed the bridge over the river with sympathetically designed entrances.

A pair of the South West Trains class 442 EMUs franchised by Stagecoach are seen near Chalton working a diverted London Waterloo to Weymouth express in March 2005. The lead unit is set 2412 named *Special Olympics*. In the opposite direction the top of a class 444 built by Siemens, which will replace the 442s can be seen.

On the main line in East Anglia, the franchise identified as One Group operated the services. In the grey livery with 'rainbow' stripes, 90003 *Raedwald* approaches Colchester with an express from Norwich bound for London Liverpool Street in February 2006. This particular engine (and for a short time 90004) carried a very dark grey bodyside, whereas all other class 90s wore the same grey as the coaching stock.

On the outskirts of Littlehampton, a Southern franchised Bombardier built class 377 approaches its destination, having started at London Victoria. The set number is 377108, and the photo was taken in April 2006. In the background, another class 377 makes its way from Brighton to Portsmouth Harbour.

On the Settle and Carlisle route, one of the ubiquitous class 66s, in this case EWS 66101, approaches the summit of the line at Ais Gill, working a Carlisle to Crewe engineers' departmental train in July 2009. The slopes of Wild Boar fell tower are on the left-hand side.

The General Electric Powerhaul class 70s are seen regularly on intermodal workings in the South of England, working services from Southampton Docks to the Midlands and North of England. Freightliner 70007 passes Mortimer in July 2011 with a Southampton Maritime Container Terminal to Manchester Trafford Park service.

One of the newer entrants to the UK scene is Colas. In their distinctive colour scheme, two of their class 66s, 66847 and 66849, pass my local station at Winchfield with an Eastleigh to Hoo Junction departmental train in February 2014. The hole in the station roof was the result of gales.

The race is on near South Kenton in September 2014, although not much of a contest! A Virgin class 370 Pendolino from London Euston to Manchester Piccadilly overtakes a London Underground Bakerloo line train from Elephant & Castle to Harrow and Wealdstone. The difference in speed will be close to 100mph!

Eurotunnel Services

Shortly before the introduction of the class 92s for hauling freight services through the Channel Tunnel (and initially passenger services although never implemented), a few French locomotives were allocated for these duties. In this rare view, SNCF 22379 stands on the English side at Cheriton, waiting for business in July 1994. The engine carries the mandatory British yellow front end for safety purposes, and also a small Railfreight Distribution decal, RFD being the designated BR Freight sector to operate these services.

Hauled by number 9008, one of the Bo-Bo-Bo locomotives specially designed for Channel Tunnel shuttle services, a lorry shuttle from Frethun to Cheriton, nears the English terminal, with a coach for lorry drivers behind the loco. The semi-open design of the lorry vehicles can just be made out. The picture was taken in March 1995, before the vegetation in the foreground had eliminated the scene.

At Frethun, a car shuttle is being loaded, with locomotive 9014 at the rear (all shuttle trains are topped and tailed). Note the size of the double deck car carrier wagons, dwarfing the locomotive in April 1995.

Travelling at full line speed of 186mph (300kph), an eighteen car class 373 Eurostar speeds through the Kent countryside in September 2010, with a mid-morning service from London St Pancras International to Paris Nord.

Ireland

One of the small General Motors diesels of class 181, formerly classified in power category B, number B181 in the CIE livery extant in June 1977, shunts a rake of wagons outside Limerick station.

Inside the works at Inchicore, Dublin, are class 001 (A) 053 and class 141 (B) 143 being serviced in the running shed part of the facility. Taken in February 1988.

The DART (Dublin Area Rapid Transit) system was introduced in 1983, using two car units manufactured in Germany by Linke Hofmann Busch. Working from Bray to Howth, 8337 and 8137 are departing from Lansdowne Road station, and are about to travel underneath one of the stands of the Rugby Union Football stadium. Photographed in April 1989.

At Drogheda, class 001 number 005 stands on the freight only branch to Tara mines and the Platin cement works, working a trainload of gypsum in December 1992. This class was built by Metropolitan Vickers in England, using Crossley diesel engines, but performance was so poor that they were re-engined with EMD 645 power.

Loco 129 of class 121 (B) hauls a push-pull set of coaches into Laytown, with a Dublin to Drogheda stopping service in December 1992. The semaphores did not have long to last before being replaced with electric signals.

A train of ballast empties, with a plough van at each end, passes Balbriggan in December 1992. Class 001 048 does all the work pulling the train up a gradient. The signalman watches over everything from his box.

Express services between Dublin Connolly and Belfast were normally powered by locomotives from Northern Ireland Railways. One such train is passing the neat little station at Rush & Lusk, headed by NIR 113 *Belfast & County Down*. The three NIR engines of class 111 were identical to the IR class 071, and named after the constituent railways that formed NIR.

The class 071s, built by EMD in 1976, were of 2,475 horsepower, giving a substantial improvement for operating purposes. Loco 086 passes the battlements at Inchicore with an eastbound train of ammonia tanks in August 1994. Note the barrier wagons at each end of the train.

Class 071 number 076, carrying the new IR logo, passes Charleville with a train load of sugar beet, destined for the processing plant at Mallow in October 1994.

A Belfast to Dublin Connolly express passes Malahide in April 1995, with NIR 112 *Northern Counties* on the front end. This station now has OHE for the extended DART system, which now serves the town.

Dramatic lighting from a lowering sun and thunderstorm clouds emphasise the colours of the latest locomotive classes on Irish Railways. Class 201 221 comes off the causeway at Malahide one evening in April 1995, working a Drogheda to Dublin stopping train. The class 201s were built by General Motors in the USA, the first 120 ton loco being flown across to Ireland in a Russian aircraft!

The tide is in at the mouth of the Delvin River near Gormanston, and a ballast train rumbles over the viaduct behind a mixed class 121 and class 141 combination. The April 1995 weather looks somewhat stormy.

Lunchtime in September 1995, and on this occasion the Belfast to Dublin express is in the hands of IR 204, which is starting away from its stop at Drogheda. This view has now changed markedly, with the cutting sides on the right cut back and extra tracks laid to provide for a maintenance depot for multiple units.

NIR bought two engines of the IR 201 class, one of which, 208, is seen exiting the viaduct over the River Boyne at Drogheda in March 1997. The colour scheme was shortly replaced by a colourful 'Enterprise' scheme, in line with renaming the Belfast and Dublin expresses with this title.

In the Enterprise colours, and somewhat off the beaten track for these colours, IR 230 enters Kildare station in September 2006, with an express from Cork to Dublin Heuston. This IR locomotive was painted in the Enterprise scheme to act as a reserve should either of the two NIR locos be unavailable.

IR 222 in the new InterCity green livery, rests at Dublin Heuston after arrival with an express from Cork in September 2006. The station gives a feeling of unhurried calm and light.

Latvia

Russian built TEP70 204 heads a four coach passenger train at Gulbene in May 2012. (Murray Lewis)

A double M62 set 2M62 0293, operated by Baltijas Tranzita Serviss, heads a tank train through the woods at Usma, near Ventspils in May 2012. (Murray Lewis)

An LDz passenger train stops at Jelgava in May 2012. Locomotive M62 1198 has been given a good clean. (Murray Lewis)

A PTG enthusiasts' tour train stands in Eglaine station. TEP70 335 carries a different colour scheme from that seen before, and towers over the coaching stock. May 2012. (Murray Lewis)

Several Eastern European countries have narrow gauge systems, this Latvian consist being typical. Standard Soviet narrow gauge diesel TU2M 273 is seen at Aluksne on the line to Gulbene. (Murray Lewis)

Lithuania

LG class CHME3 6327 stands at the head of a short passenger train at Marcinkonys in May 2013. Note that two lines of OHE are still present, but only one track exists! (Murray Lewis)

At the other end of the train is TEM2 2762, providing plenty of motive power for the three coaches. (Murray Lewis)

The class M62s can be seen in almost every country from the old Eastern Bloc days. Illustrating this, M62K EOS 1091 stands with a three coach train at a very modern looking station at Ignalina in May 2013. (Murray Lewis)

Luxemburg

Nohab 1604 stands in Luxemburg station with a passenger train in January 1991. (DC Collection)

The SNCF rolling stock of a Luxemburg to Longwy train is brought into the station by French built class 900 loco 911 in May 1991.

Of similar design to the SNCF 12000 class, CFL 3616 *Dudelange* waits for another assignment at Luxemburg station in September 1994.

Of the same design as the SNCB class 13, CFL 3010 has lowered its pantograph and waits in Luxembourg Station with the empty stock of its last working in May 2004.

Whilst waiting for its orders for new locomotives to be delivered, CFL leased some Bombardier TRAXX engines, one of which, 185 524-6, moves out of the station to go to the sidings with the empty stock.

French designed EMU 256 leaves Bettembourg with a train for Volmerange in May 2004. Not the most aesthetically pleasing of trains, I think!

Spot on time, EMU 2022 arrives at Schifflange whilst operating a train from Petange to Luxemburg. These trains are similar to the SNCF Z11500 units.

Of the same design as the SNCB class 55, CFL 1818 heads a westbound mixed freight train past Noertzange in May 2004.

The class Di 6 locos, rejected by Norway and then leased by Dispolok, found their way onto the CFL network. Illustrating one of their activities, ME 26-02 hauls an eastbound freight train past Noertzange in May 2004.

An MaK G1000 loco 1105 shunts Corail stock at Luxemburg in April 2012. Pity about the orange netting!

The new class 4000 is a standard Bombardier TRAXX design, which has taken over many duties from older classes now withdrawn. Many of the class carry advertising liveries, one of which is seen on 4006, standing in Luxemburg station, ready to depart for Wasserbillig in April 2012.

Another design is carried by 4018, which is ready to take a train to Koblenz at 1620. However, it has a long wait since the time is only 1540, but being a Sunday, there is no rush. The through services from Luxemburg through to Koblenz and onwards have now ceased, changing at Trier being required.

A stormy sky threatens double deck EMU 2209, which has stopped at Petange while on its way from Luxemburg to Athus in April 2012. Another French design similar to SNCF Z24500 class.

Netherlands

Similar to the SNCF 8100 class, the Dutch class 1100s were subsequently modified with noses for safety purposes. In the original shape, 1128 departs from Utrecht with an Amsterdam to Koln train formed of DR coaches, and is seen in June 1977.

After the cessation of the Wath to Guide Bridge services in the UK, NS obtained the six class EM2 electric locos used on this DC line. Renumbered into an NS classification, 1502 stands at Hoek van Holland ready to leave for Innsbruck as the lowering sunlight glints on the train in the evening of a day in June 1977.

In the original blue colour, 1157 has passengers boarding the train, which is a through service from Hoek van Holland to Moscow. The Sealink steamer can be seen in the port.

The 1200 class was rather a hybrid, being built by Werkspoor with Baldwin bogies and Westinghouse electrics. 1220 has just arrived at Maastricht in November 1987, with a service from Amsterdam.

Dignity and impudence at Maastricht where 'Sik' shunter 211 keeps company with 1314, one of a class similar to the SNCF 7100s.

Diesel hauled trains are in the minority in the Netherlands, but 2306 is hauling a train of large hopper type wagons south in the direction of Liege. Taken at Maastricht in November 1987.

In September 1994, the sun is out at Maastricht, and there are plenty of engines on parade. Stabled in the sidings alongside the station are representatives of classes 1100, 1200, 1300, 1600 and 6400, including locos 1214 and 1642.

At Bad Bentheim in Germany, locomotives of through trains are changed. The DB class 101 having been removed, NS 1771 *Abcaude* takes its place at the head of a two hourly Berlin to Schipol express. The bicycle is worthy of note, being used by the shunter. After uncoupling the DB engine, he cycles back to mid-train, uncouples some coaches whilst the NS loco backs on, and then cycles back to couple up the NS loco. He then retires to recover before the return working requires the same treatment! Taken in July 2002.

Three NS 6400 diesels, 6494, 6492 and 6486, amble through Oberhausen Sterk in April 2004 with a train of coal hoppers, presumably carrying coal for export via Rotterdam.

A typical example of one of the NS EMUs, with their distinctive shape, is seen at Zwijndrecht in May 2004, with Plan T unit 523 working a Roosendaal to Den Haag service.

By May 2004 open access operator ACTS has acquired the class 1200s from NS. In the new livery, 1251 with ex-SNCB diesel 6703 haul a lengthy intermodal bound for Amsterdam through the station at Amersfoort.

The class 66, introduced by the British company EWS, has been accepted in the northern part of Europe, and with its class 77 air-conditioned cousin is used by a number of companies. DLC was a private Belgian company, but one of their class 66s, PB03, is seen approaching Amersfoort from the Amsterdam direction with an intermodal service. The company has since been taken over by Crossrail.

The stylish station at Tilburg sees loco 1843 departing with a train from Den Haag for Venlo. The station provides a very convenient spot for photographers!

One of the MaK G2000 locos with the part width cab arrangement passes Tilburg in May 2004 with an intermodal service from Rotterdam. Locomotive SL2001 is operated by Short Lines.

Norway

The EL8 class was built in Germany in 1940 during the Second World War occupation, and are similar to the German class E18. Now withdrawn and lacking pantographs, 8.2059 is seen in July 1988. (DC Collection)

The Di4 class of Co-Co locomotives are powered by GM diesel engines. The train headed by 4.653, with a Nohab class Di3 behind, stands in Bodo station with a service to Trondheim, and was taken in July 1988. (DC Collection)

The EL 11 class dated from the early 1950s, one example being 11.2092, which is seen at Myrdal with the Flam train in July 1988. The main Oslo to Bergen line is behind the roofs on the left-hand side. (DC Collection)

Class Skd 220c loco 206 is stabled between duties at Bergen in June 2007.

A class BM69 EMU 69669 leaves Bergen station with a local service train to Voss, in spite of what the destination on the front of the train shows!

The EL18 class of electric locos are identical to the Swiss class 460, and operate the major express services in Norway. EL18 2255 is seen during a wet stop at Voss in June 2007, in charge of an Oslo to Bergen express.

The stylish BM73 tilting train sets are used on InterCity services, one such being seen at Bergen. Set number 73016 heads another set, and the pair will soon depart for Oslo.

Another service to Oslo stands in Bergen station, catching the afternoon sun, which brings out the colours of EL18 2249. This class is now receiving a revised livery. Taken in June 2007.

The self-contained Flambahn runs from the fjord at Flam to Myrdal. Two train sets operate the line – a major tourist attraction. Each set was topped and tailed by class EL17 locomotives. Ready to leave Flam, EL17 2227 in its green livery, is at the rear of the train.

Flam is at the end of one of the longest fjords in Norway, and the Flambahn connects with cruise ships. Not many can equal the size of Cunard line *Queen Mary 2*, which is moored at the quayside in June 2007, dwarfing everything around!

The Norwegian CargoNet company operates freight trains in Norway itself, but also into Sweden. At Kumla in Sweden, 185 712-6, leased from Railpool, heads south with an intermodal service. The strange lighting is because the photo was taken after the sun had set, and it was now a cloudy twilight, but the train was too unusual to ignore. Taken in May 2012.

Poland

In former years, Polish locomotives carried a variety of colour schemes before the present corporate sector schemes were introduced. Class EP08 006 heads a passenger train at Poznan in June 1994. (DC Collection)

In a totally different scheme, EP09 009 is also seen at Poznan on the same day in June 1994. Different schemes added to the interest in the railways. (DC Collection)

On a foul wet day in July 2005 (so much for summer!), diesel ST43 365 enters the yards at Guben (Germany) with a lengthy train of coal hoppers.

EP09 023 arrives at Bohumin in the Czech Republic with a through service from Warszawa to Wien Sud in June 2009. A CD loco will take the train on from here. Note the different livery from the previous picture of an EP09 loco.

It is August 2010 and another wet day in Poland, where EP07 1049 arrives at Wroclaw Glowny with a train from Warszawa. Classes EP07 and EU07 were derived from the British class 83.

In the new InterCity colours, EU07 316 arrives at Wroclaw Glowny on the same wet day, with a service from Krakow.

PKP Cargo EU43 004, a Bombardier TRAXX class, passes Berlin Schonefeld with a westbound freight train in August 2010, but now the sun is out!

A pair of Lotos class 146s, with 146 273-9 in front, stand in the sidings at Rzepin in May 2011. These locomotives are leased from Railpool, and carry that company's distinctive blue band.

Some class M62s were rebuilt into this rather strange looking design, and reclassified as class 311D. In a very uninspiring colour, ITL 311D-01 is seen running round at Rzepin.

The backbone of freight haulage for many years has been the class ET22. In PKP Cargo livery, ET22 1100, running wrong line, passes through the attractive station at Rzepin with a westbound intermodal service in May 2011.

In freshly applied PKP Cargo colours, EU07 1503 arrives at Rzepin with a westbound mixed freight train. In the siding, Freightliner Class 66 PL 66003 passes the day.

In 2003, the former head of Wisconsin Central, Ed Burkhardt, established operations in Poland (and Estonia). Here we see M62M 006 in Rail Polska colours running round at Rzepin in May 2011. The locomotive has been modified from the standard M62 and carries the old WC colour scheme.

Koleje Mazowieckie operate trains in the Warszawa area, but what one of its locomotives was doing in Bavaria in June 2011 is a mystery. Dead in Transit behind a Locomotion class 139, E583 004 is in a freight train passing Assling, heading towards Munchen.

In August 2012, InterCity livery is now widespread, and EP09 027 is seen at Leszno with an express from Warszawa to Wroclaw via Poznan. The modern station design does not quite blend with the overhanging lamp on the left-hand side!

The workhorse of many commuter and local train services is the class EN57 EMU. In a non-standard colour scheme, EN57 2023 arrives at Leszno with a stopping service to Wroclaw.

In 2012, Poland and Ukraine hosted the European Football Cup Final matches, and following Austria's example four years beforehand, the class 370 and some EP09 locos were painted in the colours of the last sixteen competing countries. Arriving at Poznan Glowny in August of that year, the Ukranian loco 370 004 heads an express from Berlin to Warszawa.

Almost immediately afterwards, the Polish loco 370 001 starts away from Poznan with the Warszawa to Berlin train.

Przewozy Regionalne (PR) operates a wide range of passenger services throughout Poland, apart from the InterCity trains. In the new livery adopted for its locomotives, EU07 185 arrives at Kutno with a semi-fast service from Warszawa to Poznan in August 2012.

One of the EP09s carrying the football country colours passes through Kutno with a Warszawa to Poznan express, headed by EP09 022 in the blue and white of Greece.

The yard at the PESA works at Bydgoszcz can be seen from a passing train, and in August 2012 hosted Kolprem TEM2 151, PKP InterCity EU07 106, PPMT M62 1769 and ex-ITL 232.03.

Further along at the PESA works was DLA 3E/1M-488 looking very smart.

At the far end of the works yards, stood the PESA works shunter SM42 number 2 in a unique colour scheme.

At Pszczalki, SU42 553 has stopped on its journey from Gdynia to Cjolnice. The double deck coach in the middle of the train seems out of character!

Ex-Czech class 181s are seen in several parts of Poland. At Pszczalki, Lotos 181 060-5 heads south with a tank train in August 2012.

To English eyes used to Freightliner class 66s in their standard green colours (see the picture at Rzepin with 66003 previously), it was a breath of fresh air to see FLP 66001 *Willy Brandt* arrive at Rzepin in this unique, and very striking colour scheme. The engine had arrived with a train of hoppers and was captured running round the train. Taken in August 2012.

At Rzepin, local trains from Poznan to Frankfurt (Oder) change engines from, usually, a class ET22 to an SU45 diesel in view of the different voltages between Poland and Germany. SU45 115 looks very smart in two tone green with its contrasting double deck stock.

Dramatic lighting associated with the forthcoming storm brings out the colours of 370 006 in Czech Republic colours, which is working a Berlin to Warszawa express, stopping at Poznan Glowny.

Four of the class 370s carried colours relating to the cities in Poland at which the football matches were to be played. 370 009 represents Gdansk and is seen at Poznan Glowny in August 2012 with a now defunct service from Amsterdam and Basel to Moskva, running two hours late.

Polish locomotives now range quite widely in Europe, as illustrated by a pair of ES64 F4s, 842 in the lead, heading west with an intermodal service through Payerbach Reichenau at the foot of the Semmering pass in Austria. Seen in July 2014.

Russia

TE7 054 has brought a train from Iuriev Polski to Alexandrov, where it is going to be relieved by another loco. The engine carries an attractive colour scheme and is seen in July 1992. (DC Collection)

VL10 1621 has now taken over, and will haul this lengthy train to Berendeevo. (DC Collection)

2TE10M 2640 covers the countryside with its exhaust smoke, whilst working a freight train. (DC Collection)

2TE10uT 0044 is in charge of a passenger service. (DC Collection)

Chs7 140 has arrived at Moscow Jaroslavi with a train from Alexandrov ex-Archangelsk in July 1992.
(DC Collection)

ChS7 140 passes Berendeevo with a passenger train. (DC Collection)

CHME3 1554, a Skoda built diesel locomotive, has a nine-coach train in tow at a station whose name board cannot be deciphered. (DC Collection)

ChS4T 669 is seen at Bui in July 1992 with a passenger train. Note the alternative number carried on the cab side. (DC Collection)

Sweden

Empty Pagatagen X11 EMU 3113, named *Edvard Persson,* coasts into a bay platform at Malmo Central station in September 2003 to get ready to operate a local service.

One of the X2000 tilting EMU train sets, number 2033, departs from Malmo with an express service to Stockholm in September 2003. One of these sets was trialled on the North East Corridor in the USA, back in the 1980s, as were an SNCF class 6500 and a DB ICE, preparatory to the Americans introducing their own Acela high speed train sets.

An X61 class EMU 6050 arrives at Stockholm Central with a local service in May 2012.

An X12 EMU heads out of Flemingsburg with a local service. The main line from Goteborg enters on the right.

The Rc/Rd classes have been developed over the years, including the OBB class 1043, which was the precursor of the well-established class 1044/1144s in Austria. Used on both passenger and freight services throughout Sweden, a Rail Cargo Rc4 in the old livery with RC decals ambles through Hallsberg with an eastbound mixed freight train in May 2012.

Green Cargo diesel T44 331 heads west at Hallsberg with a pair of tank wagons.

Nohab diesels are still seen quite widely, and in May 2012 at Hallsberg, Tagkraft TMX 1042 was seen trailing a train of empty log carriers.

Hector Rail has become a substantial international freight operator, using a fleet of modern locomotives such as the Bombardier TRAXX locos and, as seen here, Siemens Taurus engines. Shining in the sun, 242 531 *La Motta* works light engine at Hallsberg. Take note of the inscriptions on No. 1 end, showing the power and maximum speed of this class.

In the proper Green Cargo colours, Rc4 1296 is in charge of a westbound mixed freight train at Hallsberg.

Perhaps the most interesting class of locomotives operated by Hector Rail is the 141, originally the OBB class 1012, comprising three experimental electric engines. In the morning sunshine, HR 141 002-6 starts its journey east from Hallsberg with an intermodal service in May 2012.

SkJb operates premium passenger trains from Goteborg to Uppsala via Stockholm. In May 2012, 185 707-8, leased from Railpool, works the empty stock back to Uppsala, passing under the suspension footbridge at Hallsberg station.

SJ Rc6 1372 leads failed 1388 into Hallsberg with a late running Stockholm to Oslo express in May 2012.

Tagab Rc2 009 starts away eastbound from Kristinehamn in May 2012, with a train of empty log bolster wagons.

An X52 Regina EMU operated by VTAB leaves Kristinehamn as it commences its trip to Oslo.

Strukton Rail Nohab diesel TMY 9505 (495 05-7) runs light through Kristinehamn, carrying a passenger on the front step. Did he buy a ticket?!

TAGAB Rc2 008, still in TGOJ colours, passes through Orebro with a southbound intermodal service. May 2012.

TKAB X51-2 Regina EMU departs from Kumla in May 2012, working a Hallsberg to Orebro local service.